Embrace
the Chicken

Chapter One

Shivani played with her curry and rice. Usually she couldn't resist the chicken drumsticks melting off the bone into the thick gravy. Or the sweet-spicy smell of coconut milk and *garam masala*. But today she could barely eat a mouthful.

Why was life so complicated? It had been hard enough leaving Mumbai, her apartment and all her friends. It had taken *months* to find her way around here, to stop feeling like an outsider. She finally had a best friend. And now *this*.

She might as well get it over with. Even before she asked the question, she knew Papa's answer. *Let me be wrong this once*, she prayed.

"Matter what, Shivani?" Ma asked, in her usual broken English.

Shivani took a deep breath and put down her fork. Her parents were both staring at her. Only Anita continued eating, without a care in the world. Moving to Canada, making new friends in a new town, getting used to a whole different lifestyle—nothing seemed to bother her younger sister.

Shivani avoided looking at Ma as she spoke. "We have a school meeting tomorrow night. At eight. It's about a fundraiser. We're supposed to bring a parent. You'll come, won't you, Papa?"

Papa scratched his nose and let out a big burp. "Rupal, my dear, your cooking is to die for." He flashed a warm smile at Ma. She slapped his hand playfully.

"Papa, *please*!" said Shivani. "You're not answering my question."

"I am appreciating your mother's cooking," he said. "And you should too."

"*I* do, Ma," said Anita, taking a short break from shoveling food into her mouth. "I could kiss your hands every day."

"Hello? Fundraiser meeting?" Shivani said, frowning at her sister. "Will you come, Papa?"

"I'm sorry. I can't make it. I was happy that I could go to a few parent-teacher events this year. But I'm very busy at work these days. Your mother will have to go with you."

"No!" said Shivani. The word burst out. She glanced at Ma. The look in her eyes made Shivani want to crawl under the table and stay there. "I'm sorry, Ma. I *really* am, but there will be a lot of talking and asking questions and you... your..." Her words trailed away. The curry and rice on her plate was now a cold puddle of brown, flecked with white.

"I talk," Ma said softly. "No too good, but I am listening also."

Shivani shot a pleading look at Papa. "Please, can't you come just this once? I'll massage your scalp with oil and pull out the hairs from your ears, without complaining." Papa had a tough time getting Anita to do this, or Ma. This ought to sway him.

Papa shook his head. "It's time Ma started getting more involved with your school matters. You will both need to help her. We *all* have to settle down in Canada, and that includes Ma. You girls are learning English very well because you are around it all day. Same with me. But your mother needs to get out and meet other people. And you must be patient. I will take you up on your kind offer of hair removal, if it still stands."

Shivani sighed. Now she was stuck with a gross job, and she didn't even get what she wanted. Why did they have to immigrate to this small town where they were the *only* Indians? Where there wasn't even an Indian restaurant, let alone an Indian grocery shop? Papa had to drive Ma all the way to Toronto for her spices. They should have moved there.

"Can't Ma do all that *after* the meeting?" said Shivani, breaking the silence that hung over the dining table like a monsoon cloud.

Shivani thought of the boys she liked in her class. Ryan was cute, but he still hadn't noticed her. It was just a matter of time. If Ma came to the meeting and opened her mouth, he'd notice her, all right, and run in the other direction. No, Ma had to stay away until Shivani was sure she'd made it into the "cool" crowd.

"I come tomorrow," said Ma. "Argument finish."

"You're both horrible!" yelled Shivani. She jumped to her feet, pushed the chair back and raced to her room.

If pleading didn't work, maybe some drama would. It always did in the Bollywood movies!

Chapter Two

Lying in bed, staring at the ceiling, Shivani fumed. Why were parents always so clueless about their kids? Didn't they know that your reputation at school was *everything*? Had they ever been her age? The way they were acting, it was pretty hard to imagine.

Anita sauntered into the room.

Shivani sat up, scowling. "What do you want?"

"For you to stop behaving like an actress in a B-grade movie, to start," said Anita.

"Ha-ha. Go away and leave me alone," said Shivani.

"This is my room too," said Anita. She flicked up her glasses so hard that they bounced on her forehead and landed back on her nose, halfway down. "And why are you being so mean to Ma?"

"Mind your own beeswax," said Shivani. She'd heard her best friend, Mel (short for Melanie), say that to Christine when she tried to butt in on their conversation. Shivani immediately added the phrase to her vocabulary. It sounded so cool, so Canadian.

"You're behaving like a donkey," said Anita, running her hands along her long braid, "and it is my duty, as your sister, to get you to stop."

Shivani studied Anita. Her sister had decided to keep her hair long rather than getting it cut short like Shivani had done as soon as they'd arrived in Canada. Ma would often massage a thick green oil into Anita's hair, which was supposed to nourish it. Shivani thought the oil smelled weird, but Anita loved it.

"I'll pass, thanks," said Shivani when Ma offered to do the same for her.

Though the winter cap Ma forced her to wear when it was cold outside totally messed up her hair, Shivani had learned a few tips from Mel on how to fluff it up so it looked good for the rest of the day. Now that school was almost done for the year, caps and heavy jackets were out, thank goodness.

"Please, Anita. I can't deal with this now. It's way harder making friends in eighth grade than it is in sixth. Everyone has their own groups—people they grew up with. They rarely let outsiders in.

It's lucky Mel took me under her wing that first week, or I'd still be a loner."

Anita's face softened. She reached out and squeezed Shivani's shoulder. "It will be okay, *Didi*." Anita was the only one who called Shivani "Didi." She was the only one who could, really, since it was the Hindi word for "big sister." Shivani didn't really mind. "Next year we'll both be in the same school. You won't be lonely then."

"Thanks, but that doesn't do me any good now." Shivani was almost envious of her younger sister. Anita never got embarrassed about wearing a traditional outfit to the mall or taking Indian food for her school lunch. And she'd had no trouble making friends. She had invited a couple of them over already.

Shivani was really worried her friends wouldn't be as accepting as Anita's. But the truth was, she was too afraid to find out.

What would Mel say if she saw Shivani in a *shalwar kameez*? Or Ryan, who always hung out with the cool, well-dressed crowd? She was sure they would laugh in her face.

Shivani's cell phone pinged. She grabbed her bag and dug it out. A text from Mel.

Hey, Shivi-girl, how's it going?

"You can go now," Shivani said to Anita, dying to answer the text. Not that Anita could see the screen, but still.

Anita didn't leave but instead plonked onto her bed, humming a Bollywood tune. Shivani groaned. Having a younger sister was a pain in the butt.

"Neets!" Ma called out. "Come help me with the dishes, please."

"Ha! Saved by dirty dishes," said Anita as she slipped off the bed. "I was about to start my homework. In *our* room."

Shivani texted Mel back.

Just finished dinner. You?

> Ditto. My bro's being a pain. But
> finally went to his room. Don't
> have to see his ugly mug until
> morning.

Sis and I share a room. T-O-R-T-U-R-E

> I hear ya. You coming to the
> meeting tomorrow?

Yes.

> Who's coming with you?

Not sure. Papa is busy at work.

> Your mom back from India?
> Dying to meet her. Mom said
> she's a sweet lady.

Mel's mom was a real-estate agent and had shown them a few houses around town. Luckily, Papa had done most of the negotiations and talking. Ma had barely said a word.

Your mom is pretty cool too.

> You didn't answer me. Is your
> mom back or not?

Shivani's face grew warm even though she was alone. It had been getting harder and harder to come up with reasons why Mel couldn't meet her mother. So one day she had told Mel that her mom had gone back to India for a visit.

But if Ma turned up at the meeting the next night and they talked, Mel would know Shivani had been lying. She looked heavenward, hoping at least one of the Hindu gods would take pity on her and inspire a solution. Nothing. Were they sleeping, or on vacation? It was up to her.

Shivani could tell from the noises in the kitchen that Ma was almost finished cleaning up. Shivani couldn't face another lecture tonight. And she had to think of some way to keep Ma away from the meeting tomorrow.

Ma's back and calling me. Gotta run!

K. See ya tomorrow. Nite.

Shivani quickly changed into her pj's, flicked off the lights and crawled into bed. When the door opened, Shivani forced herself to breathe evenly.

"Already asleep, Shivi?"

Shivani lay still, her heart hammering against her rib cage. What was wrong with wanting to fit in? Why couldn't Ma, Papa and Anita understand how hard it was?

Through slitted eyes, Shivani watched her mom outlined in the doorway.

The gods must have heard her prayer this time. Ma sighed softly and stepped back. Just before she shut the door, though, she said, "I know you awake. But we talk tomorrow. Good night, Shivi."

Shivani threw off the duvet as her body burned with shame.

Chapter Three

"You have to come for a sleepover someday," said Mel.

"Cool!" said Shivani. "When?"

"I'll check with Mom and let you know. She's pretty busy with the fundraiser, but the two of us can take care of ourselves, right?"

"Right!" said Shivani, a warm glow in her chest. *This*. This is what she had to protect. If that meant little white lies now and then, so be it. She glanced over at Katya, a girl who usually sat by herself at the front of the class. Katya's fashion sense was a bit weird, and her hair changed color every week. No one ever took the seat beside her. Even at the cafeteria she had a table all to herself. But Katya didn't seem to care.

Shivani couldn't bear it if she ended up like Katya. She was sure that if any of her new friends found out how different her family was, she'd be kicked out of the cool club. So for now, Ma and her *desi*—Indian—ways had to stay hidden.

"Good morning!" said the teacher, Mrs. Glass, as she strode into the classroom. "Settle down, everyone."

The room was quiet almost immediately. You didn't mess with Mrs. Glass. She took attendance and then, leaning against the front of the desk, spoke again.

"Before we get started with today's lesson, I want to spend a few minutes talking about our upcoming fundraiser. As you know, it's a big deal for the school. I would love to hear your ideas on how we can make it really fun for everyone."

"Go-karting!" said Ryan.

Shivani pictured his lanky frame tucked into a small cart. He'd look adorable.

Mrs. Glass shook her head. "That is certainly a fun idea, Ryan, but I'm afraid it won't work. The game stalls will be set up all over the field, and the food stalls in the gym."

"How about a pie-throwing contest?" said Mel. Laughter rippled through the class. "At the teachers," she added.

For Shivani, the idea of throwing a pie at a teacher was horrifying but thrilling. Back in India, no one would *dare* make such a suggestion. "I second that!" she called out.

Mel smiled at her.

Mrs. Glass laughed. "We have tried that in the past. It's a great idea, but we must be mindful of food waste, even for a worthwhile cause. So many people around the world struggle to find enough to eat. Any other ideas?"

"Video-game challenge!" said Kylie. "I have four remote controllers and a large TV screen that my dad can set up. We can have solo games, or kids can play against one another."

"Chicken chucking!" said Dean. "We get kids to throw rubber chickens into a basket a few feet away. If they get it into the basket, they win."

"These are all good ideas," said Mrs. Glass. "What else?"

"What about a Lost and Found Fashion Show?" said Shivani, her eyes on her desk. "The contestants have to dress up with items from the lost-and-found bin."

"That's a great idea!" said Mel.

"Yes, I like that, Shivani," said Mrs. Glass, scribbling on a pad in front of her. "I'll talk to the committee about it."

Shivani smiled, her heart swelling at the compliment. By summer, she might have a few more friends. Maybe she'd even get invited to the pool parties Mel talked about. Ryan might be there too. They'd become best friends, maybe more. It was going to be a *glorious* summer.

Mel's nudge made her daydream disappear. "Earth to Shivi-girl. What were you thinking about? Spill."

"Later," said Shivani.

Mrs. Glass spent a few more minutes taking down the names of everyone who wanted to participate. Even Katya put up her hand, although no one offered to partner up with her. She said she was fine with running a stall by herself. Shivani admired her guts and made a mental note to ask Katya if she wanted to help out at their stall. She was sure Mel wouldn't mind.

"Also, a quick reminder about tonight's meeting. We will need adult volunteers for the food stalls. I'd like everyone to bring at least one adult tonight who will be willing to help at the fundraiser. They will be manning the stall and preparing the food."

"Can my friend volunteer?" asked Ryan. "Even if he doesn't go to this school?"

Mrs. Glass smiled. "Absolutely. We need all the help we can get."

"What kind of food can we bring?" asked Katya. "My mother makes great blinis. We could have savory and sweet toppings and let the customers choose."

"Sounds delicious," said Mrs. Glass. "Anything goes as long as it's nut free and kid friendly. We'll discuss all the details at the meeting tonight."

The *aloo paratha* she had eaten for breakfast started to climb Shivani's throat. If Ma offered to make Indian food, people's mouths would be in flames. She tended to go a bit heavy on the spices. Shivani vowed to work extra hard before, during and after the fair. She had to make up for the fact that her parents would not be helping out this year.

No. Way.

Chapter Four

"So can we hang out at your place after school?" Mel asked. She picked at the hummus and carrots she'd brought for lunch. "Or are you hiding some deep, dark secret you don't want me to find out about?"

"Don't be silly," said Shivani. She took a bite of her cheese sandwich and chewed slowly, trying to buy time.

At school some of her classmates still peeked at her lunch and then looked away when they saw it was just a sandwich. Other kids brought "different" foods from home like cabbage rolls, fried rice or pirogies. But Shivani wanted to fit in, not stand out. The *samosas* stayed at home.

Mel was starting to insist on coming to her house. It was only fair, given that Shivani had been to Mel's place so often. Not once had Shivani invited her over. But how could she bring her new best friend to her small house, have her see the tiny room she shared with her sister? Mel's house was much larger than hers and beautifully decorated. And she and her brother had their own rooms.

But it wasn't really her house that bothered her so much. Shivani dreaded Mel meeting Ma. Her mom couldn't speak a full sentence of proper English!

She even threw in Hindi words when she couldn't think of the right English word. So *embarrassing*.

"How about today?" said Mel. "We can do our homework together and then come back to the school after dinner for the meeting. I'll tell Mom I'll meet her back here."

Shivani almost choked on a bite of her sandwich. "Sorry, Mel, but we can't do it this week. Ma is really busy. Maybe next week?"

"You *always* say that," said Mel, frowning. "Seriously, is there something you're not telling me? You know BFFs shouldn't keep secrets from each other."

Shivani forced out a laugh. "You need to cut back on the mystery novels, Mel. I'm not hiding anything. Hey, what did you think about Ryan saying he'd bring his friend to help out?"

The distraction worked. "If he's as much of a dish as Ryan," said Mel,

"I should arrange to have their stall right next to ours."

"You could do that?" said Shivani. "How?"

The bell rang.

"Come over after school and I'll explain," said Mel. "We also need to decide what stall we want. They have to finalize the sign-up sheet tonight."

Shivani sighed in relief. But how long could she keep putting Mel off with these lies? *Just a bit longer*, she told herself. Just until the summer holidays. Then she wouldn't be the new kid anymore.

"Can't wait," said Shivani. They hurried back to class.

At Mel's house, Shivani slurped the last of her chocolate milkshake. It slid down her throat, sweet and thick. She loved North American food. Not that there was anything wrong with the food she got at home. She just didn't get a chance to eat things like burgers and fries as often as she liked. Ma was a strict vegetarian and didn't allow any beef in the house. She did cook chicken for the rest of the family, as well as fish. But never beef. Shivani had to admit it was great that Ma let her and Anita choose what they ate outside the house though.

Mel's mom walked into the kitchen. Shivani had first met Mrs. Jennings when she'd driven her family around to look at houses. She'd mentioned that she had a daughter the same age as Shivani and promised she would help Shivani settle in. And sure enough, Mel had walked up to her on the first day of school and introduced herself. They'd gotten along right from the start.

"How are you all enjoying your new home?" Mrs. Jennings asked.

"It's good, although I wish I had my own room," Shivani said, trying not to sound too ungrateful.

"Well, you never know," Mrs. Jennings replied. "Maybe your parents will upgrade. With that location, your house has great resale value."

Shivani smiled politely. How was that going to help her *now*? She needed her space. Anita was always butting in or hanging around at the wrong time. Which was pretty much *all* of the time.

"Is your mother settling in all right?" Mrs. Jennings asked. "Tell her I'd be happy to introduce her to some of my friends. It's much easier to get used to a new place when you have support from the community."

"Like me," said Mel. "I'm very supportive."

"Modesty runs in our family," Mrs. Jennings said, rolling her eyes. "Can you tell, Shivani?"

Shivani smiled. "I think Mel is awesome."

"Thank you, Shivi-girl. I think you are awesome too! Shivani's mom just got back from India," said Mel, turning to her mother. "And Shivani has promised to invite me over soon. So I'll tell Mrs. Das myself about your offer. Hey! Maybe we can have them over for dinner one night!"

The thought of that made Shivani's gut clench. "Sure, but for now maybe we can get going on that fundraiser stuff," she said, hoping to change the subject.

Upstairs, Mel flung herself on the bed. Shivani stood by the door. She couldn't help but feel jealous every time she entered Mel's room. The walls were a pale yellow, and the duvet on the bed was covered in sunflowers. Matching yellow curtains gave the room a cheery look. *I'd be so much happier if I had my own room,* she thought. *Especially if it was the color of sunshine.*

The walls in her room were moss green. It was the color that had been on sale at the Home Depot. Papa had bought enough to paint the entire house. It wasn't too bad. On rainy days she felt she was in the middle of the forest. But yellow or even a sky blue would have been nicer. She had asked Anita about pooling their allowances so they could paint their room a brighter color. But Anita had refused, saying the green was fine and there was no point wasting money.

"You have that look on your face again," said Mel, throwing a pillow at her. "Stop with the daydreaming already."

Shivani snapped out of it. "Hey, what do you think of Ryan?"

"He's okay."

"Just okay?" said Shivani, raising her eyebrows.

"When you've grown up with someone, it's not easy to see them as boyfriend material."

"Good. Then I don't have to share him with you."

Mel yawned. "All yours. And I think he likes you too."

"Seriously?" Shivani said, her pulse thumping in her ears like a Bollywood beat. "Isn't he with Rhea?"

"I think that's over," said Mel. "You have a good chance, and he's a nice guy. I could arrange something for the right reward."

Shivani groaned. "Stop teasing. What?"

"I'll let you know," said Mel. "But when I call in the favor, you have to do it, right?"

Shivani nodded. "Right."

"Okay, so let's talk fundraiser," said Mel.

"I have a ton of ideas, and I've writ—"

Mel held up a hand. "I'm sure they're all good, but we're in it to win it. I have a pretty good idea which stalls attract the most crowds and make the most money."

"So which one should we do?" asked Shivani.

"I think our best bet is balloon darts," said Mel. "The Baker sisters usually grab that one every year. But if we head to the gym early tonight, get there before the doors open, we can be first in line and sign up before they can."

"Sounds good," said Shivani. "But your mom is on the committee. Can't she reserve that stall for us?"

Mel shook her head. "Mom believes everyone should have a fair chance. We'll have to line up like the rest and take our chances."

"I think she's right," said Shivani.

"But what she *can* arrange is where the stalls are placed," said Mel, her eyes sparkling.

"Meaning?"

"Whatever stall Ryan and his friend choose, their stall will be next to ours."

"Your mom's fantastic!" said Shivani.

"Hey, what about me? I'm the one who will do the begging."

"You're fantastic too!" Shivani said, hugging Mel.

Shivani's cell phone rang in her bag. She glanced at Mel's clock by the window—quarter to six. She knew who it was even before she dug out her phone. Ma refused to text her, even though Shivani had said she preferred it.

"Hi, Ma. Yes, I'm at Mel's. I told you this morning. I didn't? Of cour— okaaay, *fine*. I'll come home now."

Mel hovered close by, but Shivani turned away from her. Ma spoke mostly in Hindi. Shivani was careful to answer only in English.

"Let me say hi," Mel whispered in Shivani's ear, trying to grab the phone.

Shivani moved away. "Got it, Ma. I'm coming."

"Hi, Mrs. Das!" Mel yelled out. "When can I come over?"

In a panic, Shivani ended the call. She hoped Ma wouldn't call back. "Stop it!"

"What?" said Mel. "Just trying to be friendly. You're so stingy with an invite, I thought I'd get one directly from the head honcho."

Shivani loved Mel's attitude, but sometimes she went too far. "I have to go home. Ma's throwing a fit."

"That sucks. Didn't you tell her you were coming to my place?"

Shivani shrugged. She knew that if she had told Ma she was going to Mel's she would have gotten another lecture about inviting Mel over. Ma wanted to meet all *her* friends since Anita's friends had started coming by.

"K, then see you at the school," said Mel. "Don't be late. I don't want to be hanging outside the gym on my own like a loser."

"Sure," said Shivani, wondering how she was going to slip out after dinner without Ma noticing.

Shivani raced all the way home. Cutting off Ma's call had been a bad idea.

Breathless, she turned the key in the lock. The door was yanked open from the inside, and Ma stood there, hands on her hips, glaring at her.

"You stop line when I am *talking*?" said Ma. "In middle of talking? Bad!"

"I'm sorry, Ma," Shivani replied. "I dropped the phone, and it must have disconnected. I thought it was better if I just came straight home."

Ma's expression clearly said she wasn't buying it. "Was that Mela, wanting to come to our house?"

"Yes, Ma, and the name's Melanie." *God*, Ma couldn't even get her friend's name right!

"Why she not come here already? You go there all time. Bad manners."

From the corner of her eye, Shivani noticed Anita hovering outside their room. She was Ma's pet and sure to take her side against her sister. Shivani couldn't count on her support.

"Can you just stop lecturing me, Ma?" Shivani said. "I'm tired of being treated like a child."

She pushed past Anita, stomped into her room and slammed the door shut.

Chapter Five

Shivani did not come out of her room for dinner. She was surprised that no one came to get her. Not that she was hungry. The snacks at Mel's place had filled her up. But the unmistakable whiff of fresh *jalebis* made her mouth water. Ma could have at least called her for dessert! She knew she was being unreasonable, expecting Ma to make the first move. After all, she, Shivani, was the one who had been rude.

Still. Jalebis!

Someone knocked on the door. It couldn't be Anita. She would just barge in. It might be Papa coming to talk to her about her attitude. She couldn't ignore him. "Come in," she said reluctantly.

It was Ma. And she was carrying a bowl. A lump formed in Shivani's throat. In some ways, Ma knew her so well.

Ma held out the bowl, and Shivani took it without saying a word. The delicate orange coils of fried dough glistened with sugar syrup. Saliva flooded Shivani's mouth as she smelled the rose water.

"Thanks, Ma," she said, breaking off a large piece with her fingers and popping it into her mouth. The sweetness spread over her tongue as she crunched it up. "You are the best."

"Shivani, we talk," said Ma, sitting on the bed and patting the spot beside her. "Please, now."

Her mouth full, Shivani sat down beside Ma. The least she could do after Ma had been so nice was listen to her.

"You don't forget India because you come Canada, Shivi," said Ma. "Don't forget self, what is in your heart." She tapped Shivani's chest with a finger. "No shame about your culture, your tradition. It is good, very rich. *Special*."

"I'm not special, Ma!" Shivani said. "I'm just an outsider trying to fit in with all the kids who grew up here!"

"It take time," said Ma. "So what? You call friend here. She like you, me, Anita, Papa. Soon you have many friends."

Shivani chewed the last bit of jalebi, trying to choose her words carefully.

"My friend loves burgers," said Shivani. "You don't cook beef."

"I make samosas and chutney to die for," said Ma, kissing her fingertips like Papa always did. "All neighbors in Mumbai line up for them. No one even *remember* cow after a taste of my samosa."

Who cared about the neighbors in India? They were here in Canada now. "Mel won't like Indian food," Shivani said.

"How you know?" said Ma, her tone sharp as she stood up. "You never take paratha or curry rice to school."

"I just know, okay?" Shivani's temper was rising again, but she held her tongue. "And cold curry doesn't taste good. There's too long a lineup to use the microwave in the cafeteria."

Ma sighed and shook her head. "Get ready, Shivi. Almost time for funding in school meeting. Anita and I come with you."

"It's called a fundraiser, Ma," said Shivani. "But we're not going. I already told them you couldn't help." Shivani felt smaller than a flea, but this was no time for backing down. She still planned to slip out as soon as Ma started watching her favorite TV program. Mel would be so mad if she was late.

Ma smiled. It wasn't friendly. "Okay. You stay. Anita will take me your school. She know the way."

She turned and left the room. Shivani caught a glimpse of her sister's grinning face just outside the door. *Traitor!*

"Okay, I'm coming," said Shivani. Better she was there to do damage control than let Ma loose at the school gym with all the parents. But this meant she couldn't go early. If she did, every parent arriving would want to talk to Ma. Or Ma would try talking to them, or to Mel. No. Way. Mel would have to wait in line alone.

Sorry, Mel. I'm so sorry.

Chapter Six

The gym was almost full when they arrived. Shivani had delayed as long as she could. She had told her mom she had an important assignment to finish. She thought that if they got there just as the meeting started, there would be no time for chitchat. And once the meeting was over, Shivani planned to race out of there, using the same excuse.

With any luck, she'd get Ma in and out with very few stops.

Ma had finally called out that she wasn't waiting any longer. Shivani had raced out of the room to find her mom and Anita giggling near the door. *God help me*, she thought. She corrected herself. *No, don't. Your sense of humor is worse than Ma's, and you're sleeping on the job.*

A couple of friends waved to Shivani as she, Anita and Ma grabbed seats in the last row. There was no sign of Mel. After she'd ignored five texts from Mel, each one angrier than the last, they'd stopped. Shivani wasn't looking forward to seeing her. No doubt they would have a fight. But what else could she have done?

Ma was wearing a black blouse and a dark-blue cotton sari with a black border. She'd draped a multicolored shawl over her shoulders. In the sea of black, beige and navy spring jackets, she stood out like a peacock among crows. No matter what the weather, Ma refused to give up her traditional clothing. Shivani could feel people staring at them. She wanted to melt into the floor of the gym. *Start the meeting already!*

"We can't stay long, Ma," said Shivani. "I have to finish that assignment. It's due tomorrow."

Ma glanced around, her eyes sparkling. "So many peoples want to help with funding. Very nice. We help too."

"Our school is having one at the beginning of next year," said Anita. "I've already signed you up, Ma."

"Okeydokey," said Ma. She'd heard this word on TV and used it whenever she could, saying she liked that it rhymed.

"I already told my teacher you're too busy to volunteer," said Shivani, glaring at Anita. Why did her sister always have to do exactly the opposite of what she did?

Anita was deliberately trying to make her look bad.

Ma ignored Shivani, turned to the woman next to her and smiled. The woman smiled back.

Don't say a word, Shivani prayed silently. *Please!*

"Hello, my name Rupal Das. What your good name?"

"Nice to meet you," said the woman. "I'm Nina Petrova, Katya's mother. I *love* your shawl."

Katya, sitting on the far side of her mother, leaned forward and waved. Shivani waved back.

"Thank you." Ma opened her large purse and started rummaging inside it. "You like biscuit?"

Katya's mother looked surprised, but nodded. "Sure."

Oh no! Didn't Ma realize Mrs. Petrova was just being polite? In one evening, Ma was going to destroy the image Shivani had spent weeks building. Ma opened a small tin and offered a *jeera* biscuit to Mrs. Petrova. A hint of cumin and butter filled the air.

"Ma, please! No food or drink in the gym," Shivani said through clenched teeth. What was it with Ma and food? Everywhere she went, she carried snacks in her giant bag. She believed offering food to strangers was the best way to break the ice. Shivani had tried to explain to her many times that in Canada you didn't do things like that. But Ma refused to listen. Funny how the people she offered it to had no objections and usually asked for seconds.

Mrs. Petrova took one and bit into it. "Oh, this is delicious! You must give me the recipe, Rupal."

"Yes, yes. You come home. I show you," Ma said.

Mrs. Petrova nodded. "And I'll give you the best recipe for *pryaniki* ever."

"That cookie name?" said Ma.

She nodded. "Yes, it's a Russian spice cookie."

"In India, Priya is girl's name. It means 'loved one.'"

"Well, I do love *this* cookie!" They both laughed.

"Looks like our mothers have hit it off," said Katya, smiling shyly.

Shivani had never seen Katya smile before. Returning the smile, Shivani replied, "If you don't have a partner for the stall, you can come help Mel and me. Okay?"

Katya nodded, her cheeks warm with color. Shivani felt a glow in her chest. She knew she was being mean to Ma, but maybe she could make up for it some other way.

The principal, Mr. Travers, arrived, and the buzz died down. He got up on the stage along with the other teachers. Ma tucked the biscuit tin back into her bag.

Shivani scanned the crowd but couldn't see Mel. She would probably be up front with Mrs. Jennings. *Good*. Shivani could sneak out with Ma and Anita as soon as the meeting ended and deal with Mel's meltdown later.

"Thank you all for joining us today." The principal's voice boomed around the gym. "I see a lot of familiar faces and a few new ones. Welcome! It is because of *your* efforts that our school continues to flourish year after year. I hope this year is even better than the last!"

Shivani could see by Ma's expression that she was concentrating hard. "What he say, Anita?" Ma said in a loud whisper.

Shivani saw Mrs. Petrova glance at Ma. Why was Ma making it so obvious that she couldn't understand English very well? Why couldn't she just listen quietly and ask questions at home?

Papa would never have embarrassed her like this. Shivani couldn't wait for the meeting to end.

Principal Travers introduced Mel's mom, who stood up to a huge round of applause.

"Welcome, everyone! As many of you know, I'm Cherie Jennings. I am this year's chair of the Fundraiser Planning Committee. For those who are new, I look forward to getting to know you. Together we are going to make this the best year ever!"

More applause. It was clear that Mrs. Jennings was popular in the school and the community. Could she and Ma really be good friends? They were as different as a slice of bread and an aloo paratha.

"That is Didi's best friend's mother," whispered Anita.

"You make us meet, Shivani?"

"No, Ma," said Shivani. "We are leaving as soon as the meeting is over. I already told you, I have to study for a test and finish my assignment."

"Okay, you go. I come later. But I tell you now, you behave not nicely."

Shivani's stomach knotted. Her heart ached. She knew she was hurting Ma, but what choice did she have? If they laughed at Ma today, they'd be laughing at *her* tomorrow. She couldn't bear it, for her or her family.

"I'll be passing around the sign-up sheet soon," Mrs. Jennings said. "Please write down your name, email address and phone number. For those of you volunteering to bring food, thank you! I will be in touch with you in the next few days to discuss menu items and quantities. We will reimburse you for the cost of the ingredients."

"So, Rupal, will you be volunteering?" asked Mrs. Petrova.

"I look," said Ma. "Very busy time for me."

"One last thing before you sign up," Mrs. Jennings continued. "I've created a handout that lists the ingredients to avoid because of known allergies in our school. This includes all nuts and *especially* peanuts. We would love to have a variety of vegan, vegetarian and gluten-free options as well. If you are able to prepare those, please note that on the sign-up sheet."

"What she say?" asked Ma. "What vegan?"

"Let's go, Ma," said Shivani. "How does it matter to you? You're not making anything."

Ma glared at Shivani. "I am not hearing even *squeak* from you. Undersit?"

"*Understand*, Ma," said Anita gently. "Vegan means no animal products. So not even milk or honey. Only plant-based foods."

"Okeydokey," said Ma. "Now I understand."

The buzz in the gym started to rise again. A few parents asked questions. A committee member walked around with the handouts. Before Shivani could say anything, Ma snagged one. She folded it into a tiny neat square and tucked it into her bag.

Shivani's pulse raced. The meeting was over, and the sign-up sheet was making its way to the back. Parents started to drift around, catching up with others. Any minute now Mel would spot Ma in her colorful shawl and come over.

"Ma, I'm not feeling too well," said Shivani. "We have to go. I don't want to throw up in the gym."

Ma looked at Shivani with concern. "Okeydokey," she said softly. "We go."

"If you have to leave, Rupal, I can put your name down on the sign-up sheet," Katya's mom said. "You can get in touch with Cherie later with the rest of the details."

"Maybe next time," Ma replied. "Nice to meet you."

"Same here," she replied, holding out her hand. "And don't forget the cookie recipe."

Ma clasped Mrs. Petrova's hand in both of hers. "Of course. You welcome my home, any time. And you bring Priya."

"Pryaniki," Mrs. Petrova corrected.

They both laughed.

"I'll see you at class tomorrow," said Katya to Shivani. "You were serious about letting me help?"

"Absolutely," said Shivani. Though she wasn't as sure now about how Mel would react to this news.

But first things first.

She grasped Ma's arm and tugged. Ma sighed but followed. Just as they reached the gym doors, Shivani heard someone calling her name. Mel.

Shivani burst through the doors as fast as she could, praying Ma hadn't heard anything.

Chapter Seven

Papa was home by the time they got back. Shivani tried to escape to her room, but Ma stopped her.

"Wait, Shivani. You are rudeness today."

Ma had used her full name. She was in trouble.

"Ma, I told you not to come to the meeting, but you insisted. And then you were handing out biscuits and trying to embarr—"

"That's enough, Shivani," said Papa sternly. "What happened, Rupal?"

"My daughter shame of me!" said Ma. Her voice wobbled. Shivani felt worse than ever. "She pull me home like puppy on string."

"Is that true, Shivani?" said Papa, folding up the paper he had been reading. "We did not raise our children to disrespect their parents and elders. I'm very disappointed."

"I just don't want Ma to embarrass me in front of my friends. Is that too much to ask?" Shivani knew this was a pointless argument, but she had to say something.

"How I embarrass you if I want to help funding?" Ma said.

"Because you can't speak or understand English. But you still go having conversations with other parents.

You always make me and Anita work hard so you can be proud of us. Why don't *you* practice what you preach?"

"What mean?" said Ma.

Papa explained to Ma in Hindi. Shivani could tell he was really angry.

Ma took a deep breath. She dropped her bag on the coffee table and sat down on the sofa. She stared at her hands. For a minute no one said anything. Then Anita sat beside Ma and hugged her.

"It's okay, Ma," whispered Anita. "You take as much time as you need to learn English. I'll help you."

Finally Ma looked up. Her eyes were bright with tears. "My family—big. Seven brothers and sisters. We not have money to send everyone to school. So I fall out grade eight."

Shivani looked at the floor.

"You lucky your papa and I make enough money to let you study in private school in India. Bring you to Canada."

"And we work hard to get top marks," said Shivani. She knew she should just stop talking. But she couldn't seem to help talking back.

"You're acting like a donkey, Didi," said Anita. "For once, shut up and listen."

"*You* shut up!" Shivani snapped.

"Anita, why don't you go to your room," Papa said. "We need to have a chat with your sister."

"*I'm* proud of you, Ma," said Anita. She gave Shivani a dirty look and walked into the bedroom.

"Sit down, Shivani," said Papa, taking Anita's place beside Ma.

Shivani plunked down on the sofa. When he used that tone, it was best not to argue.

"Do you know how hard your mother and I have worked to bring us all here for a better life? I worked three jobs in India, and your mother packed tiffin lunch boxes for office workers. We even had to borrow money from relatives. Your mother could have used the money she earned for *her* education. We always talked about her going back to school once you girls were older. But you both always came first."

Shivani stared at her mother. She had had no idea Ma wanted to go back to school.

Papa continued as he clasped Ma's hand in his. "If she had put *her* needs before the family's, we wouldn't be here right now."

Shivani's throat felt tight. Her parents, but especially Ma, had sacrificed so much for her. She jumped up and hugged Ma. The familiar aroma of ginger, garlic and cloves enveloped her. "I'm so, so *sorry*, Ma. Can you ever forgive me?"

Ma kissed her forehead. "Shivi, you must think before talk. No hurt anyone, especially family. We love you—always. And you do same to us."

Shivani nodded. "I will, Ma. I get it. And I'm truly grateful."

"So I help at funding and make *you* proud," said Ma.

Shivani was torn. On the one hand, she still didn't want Ma to be there. On the other, she knew how much Ma wanted to be a part of her new life.

"Okay, Ma, but could you do me a favor, please? It would mean a lot to me."

"What, Shivi?"

"Can you help someone else out instead of cooking a dish yourself?"

"You don't like my food?" asked Ma.

"*I* love it, but I don't know—"

"You scared of peoples and what they think."

"I'm not scared," said Shivani. "I *know*. The kids in this school have very

North American tastes. Whenever they serve cabbage rolls in the cafeteria, every student complains of the smell. I don't want them to make fun of my family, or my food, but *especially* you. Can you understand that, Ma?"

Ma shook her head. She clearly did *not* understand.

"How would you know they dislike our food if you've never let them try it?" Papa said. "If you *embrace* your culture proudly, so will others. Anita still wears her shalwars, and she's invited friends over. I never see you wear yours, even at home. And we've never met any of your friends."

"I find jeans and T-shirts more comfortable," Shivani said. "And Mel's too busy helping her mother with the fundraiser." She hoped Ma wouldn't remember Mel yelling on the phone, asking for an invite. "I'll call her over when summer holidays start. Okay?"

Ma's eyes held hers. Shivani knew she wasn't fooled, not even for a second.

"So you won't ask for your own stall, right?"

"You no tell me what I do," said Ma. "Good night, Shivani."

Shivani shuffled to her room. She felt terrible. She knew she had hurt Ma this evening. And she had let Mel down. But at least now the truth was out in the open. She had apologized, and she knew Ma would never do anything to hurt her. There was nothing to worry about now. It was over.

Chapter Eight

"You stood me up, Shivani," said Mel. "I had to wait in line all by myself! *And* you ignored my texts and pretended not to hear me when I called out to you after the meeting. *Why?*"

They were in class, waiting for the teacher to arrive. Shivani wished he'd hurry up so she didn't have to have this conversation right now. It was getting worse by the minute. Lies always made things so complicated. She hated lying to her best friend. But the consequences of telling the truth would be worse.

"I'm sorry, Mel, but I-I was feeling sick. I had to get to a bathroom fast."

Mel looked at Shivani. "We have bathrooms in the school, in case you had forgotten. But that still doesn't explain why you didn't come early. Don't you want to run the stall with me?"

"I'm sorry," said Shivani. "Something came up."

"What?" said Mel.

Mel was not going to let this drop. Shivani's stomach felt queasy. "Can we please talk about this later?"

Katya walked in just then and stopped at their table. "Thanks for offering to let me join your stall, Shivani, but I found a partner yesterday. I'm all set."

"Great," said Shivani weakly.

"On top of everything else, you invite Katya to join us without asking me?" Mel said loudly. Many class-mates stared at her and Mel. "Worst friend *ever*!" Mel picked up her bag and moved to the front of the class.

Shivani spent the next hour staring at the back of Mel's head. She watched Mel whisper to the boy beside her, Alex. She didn't turn around even once.

After class Mel picked up her bag and walked out without a backward glance. By the time Shivani got to the cafeteria, Mel was already sitting at a table with some friends. There was no room for Shivani. She sat alone and tried to choke down her lunch. She knew she should go over and talk to Mel. But it was so hard. The longer their fight continued, the harder it would be to make up.

"Are you okay?"

Shivani looked up from her food. It was Katya. "Yeah, I'm okay," she said.

"Can I sit here?" Katya asked.

Shivani nodded, grateful for the company.

"Did you and Mel have a fight?" asked Katya, digging into her home-made lunch of sausage and some kind of potato. It smelled delicious.

Shivani shrugged. "Sort of."

"Hope it wasn't because you asked me to help at your stall," said Katya. "I know I'm not the most popular person in class." She laughed.

Shivani stared at her. "It doesn't bother you? Having no friends?"

Katya put down her fork. "There's a difference between real friends and those who pretend to be. I don't have time for those who make themselves look good by making others look bad. Real friends accept you just the way you are. I had a good friend at this school, but she moved away. So now I'm waiting for the right one to show up."

Why had Shivani never realized how smart and sweet Katya was? She had never bothered to look beyond the strange clothing and the purple hair. She'd been just like everybody else, desperately trying to be "normal."

"Mel's a nice girl," said Katya. "I've never heard her say anything mean about anyone. If you two are having a problem, you should talk it out before it's too late."

"You're right," said Shivani. She'd been so miserable without her best friend, and it hadn't even been a day! There was only one way to fix it. The truth. "Thanks, Katya."

After school Shivani caught up with Mel outside the main doors. "Hey, Mel, can I talk to you for a second?"

"What is it?" said Mel. Her voice was still cold.

"How about we walk to my place while I tell you what an idiot I've been."

Mel's eyes widened. "You mean, right now? Really?"

Shivani nodded.

"Let me text my mom and tell her where I'll be." Mel's fingers flew over the keyboard. "Okay, now spill—*everything*."

"You were right when you said I was trying to avoid you after the meeting. And I arrived late on purpose. I'm so, *so* sorry."

"I knew it! But why?"

Shivani looked down at the leaf-littered road. She took a deep breath, then looked up at Mel, aware that her face was burning. "Ma doesn't speak English very well."

"So?"

"She misuses words," said Shivani, sweat dripping from her armpits. "She even makes up words! I didn't want her making a fool of herself if other parents tried to talk to her."

"Is she fluent in your language… Hindu?" Mel asked.

"Hindi," said Shivani. "Yes, of course!"

"So if *I* were to learn Hindi and speak to your mom in *her* language, I'd probably stumble a lot. Would you hide me away in a closet and refuse to be seen with me?"

Shivani shook her head.

"So why would you expect your mother to be fluent in a language that is not her own? There's nothing wrong with not speaking it well. At least she's trying. None of us here are trying to communicate with *her* in Hindi."

Shivani stared at her. Put this way, it made so much sense. But Shivani remembered parties back home where a few "foreign-returned" ladies, ones who had been educated in England and then came back to India, had laughed at Ma when she tried to speak English. If Indians could be so mean to their own, what would Canadians be like? She didn't want to find out. She refused to be the laughing stock of the school before she'd had a chance to settle in.

Mel placed a hand on her shoulder. "Trust me, it won't be as bad as you think." She looked at Shivani, her eyes widening. "Wait a minute. Is *that* why you've never invited me to your place?"

Shivani nodded, hoping the tears pricking her eyelids wouldn't escape. It would be so uncool to start crying in public.

"Dumb reason, but I forgive you," said Mel. "Because that's what friends do."

"Hey! Wait up!"

Shivani froze as she recognized the voice. Mel turned back and waved.

"Where are you girls headed?" said Ryan.

"Shivani's place," said Mel. "We have an assignment to finish for tomorrow."

Ryan was looking at Shivani, and her legs started to melt. "You both volunteering for the fundraiser?"

"My mom's on the committee," said Mel, rolling her eyes. "Can you see me getting away with sitting at home while everyone works hard?"

"I'm running the archery booth," said Ryan. "It's fun teaching kids how to use a bow and arrow. And the food stalls look like they're going to be awesome too. Can't wait to pig out."

Shivani took the opportunity to ask an easy question. "So what's your favorite food?"

"Steak and potatoes," said Ryan. "Oh, and hot dogs, pizza, burgers—

guess I can't answer that kind of question when I'm hungry."

"What about Indian food?" said Mel. "Shivani's mom is a great cook."

Shivani turned to look at Mel. *Stop it*, she mouthed.

"I tried Indian food in Toronto once, when I was visiting cousins," said Ryan. "A bit too spicy for me. Maybe my taste buds aren't used to it. But it could also have been my cousin pranking me. I think he ordered the hottest version of the curry." He shrugged.

Mel dug an elbow into Shivani.

"Well, you're just going to have to try my mom's curry," said Shivani. "Maybe during the summer holidays?"

"That would be *awesome*," said Ryan. "We could hang out, maybe go to a movie."

Shivani nodded. "Sounds good." Like it was no big deal. *Oh my god!*

"Okay, gotta run," said Ryan.

He said he wants to try Ma's curry!

"So what should I call your mother?" asked Mel.

Shivani dropped back to earth with a thud. They were almost home. The moment of truth. Would she still have a friend by the end of the day? Or had she just made the biggest mistake of her life?

Chapter Nine

"Ma, I'm home!" said Shivani as she shut the door behind them. She turned to Mel with a tentative smile. "She must be in the kitchen, preparing dinner. We need to take our shoes off."

Mel slipped her boots off as she sniffed the air. "It smells *so* good in here. What is she cooking?"

"Yellow-lentil dal, jeera pulao and masala okra," said Shivani.

Mel stared. "Wow! You know all that just from sniffing the air?"

Shivani laughed. "That and I helped her shop for groceries on Sunday."

Mel punched her shoulder. "Cheater!"

"Hello, *beta*, you snack before you do work-home?" said Ma, wiping her hands on a towel as she came out of the kitchen. She froze when she saw Mel.

Mel came forward, hand outstretched. "Hello, Mrs. Das, I'm Mel. I've heard so much about you from Mom. It's so nice to finally meet you."

Ma shook her hand with a big smile. "Welcome to our house. Please to call me Aunty. You will stay for dinner, no?"

"I will stay for dinner, yes!" said Mel, grinning. "Thanks, Aunty."

"Nice. Nice," said Ma. "You go work. I bring *chai* and biscuits."

"Ma, you don't have to."

"I'm starving," said Mel, smiling at Ma. "Yes, please."

An hour later they'd finished their homework. There wasn't a crumb left on the plate of biscuits, and their mugs of chai were empty. "Delish," said Mel.

Downstairs, Shivani heard the clink of plates and a murmur of low voices. Anita was home. Papa would arrive shortly. Then they would all be sitting at the table. Eating Indian food. And *talking*. Despite how well the afternoon had gone, Shivani was nervous.

Mel checked her phone. Shivani daydreamed about her possible movie date with Ryan. It seemed like just seconds later that Ma called, "Shivani, dinner is ready."

Well, here goes nothing. If Mel didn't like the food or her family, at least she'd tried. Shivani remembered what Katya had said. *Real friends accept you just the way you are.*

Shivani introduced Mel to Papa and Anita. So far, so good. Then she helped bring the rest of the dishes to the table. Mel offered to help too. Once they sat down, Ma insisted on serving Mel first. Shivani watched nervously as Ma piled rice on Mel's plate. She smothered it with a big scoop of dal and heaped some okra beside it. She topped it with a dollop of ghee and a crisp *pappadam*. A meat-loving girl had just been served a completely vegetarian meal. This was not going to go well.

"Eat, please, before it catching cold."

Mel scooped up a large forkful and put it in her mouth. Her eyes popped open.

Shivani wanted to duck under the table. "So, um, do you like it?" she asked.

Mel shook her head and chewed furiously.

Shivani met Ma's eyes. She looked the way Shivani felt. Maybe *now*

Ma would believe her when she kept saying her friends would not like Indian food!

Mel finally swallowed that first bite and sat back. "Wow! It's *so* good, Aunty! A million flavors exploding on my tongue. So mad at you, Shivi-girl, for keeping this from me for so long!"

Ma laughed. "My nickname for her also Shivi."

"Great minds think alike!" said Mel.

Mel finished everything on her plate and asked for seconds. Ma couldn't stop smiling. Even the conversation flowed well. Papa made his usual corny jokes. Ma and Anita piped in now and then. Shivani could tell Mel was enjoying every bit of it. Including the jalebis Ma served for dessert.

"I have died and gone to heaven," said Mel after her second helping. "Best dessert ever!"

"Thank you, beta," said Ma.

"What does beta mean?" Mel asked. "Like, 'honored guest'?"

We all laughed.

"It is an affectionate term for our children, Mel," said Papa. "But we hope that you will be our guest again soon."

"I will *definitely* be back. Especially if Aunty is cooking!"

When dinner was over, Shivani walked Mel outside. She wasn't sure how to say how grateful she was. She decided to keep it simple. "Thanks!"

"For what?" said Mel. "I should be thanking *you*. Your family is fantastic, and your mom is adorable. You need to stop hiding her away."

"Mel, just because *you* like her doesn't mean everyone else will be kind. Back home, her supposed *friends* made fun of her. I was happy when Ma stopped inviting them over."

"Your ma is a strong woman, and she can take care of herself," said Mel. "And yes, there will always be some idiots who are afraid of anything different. But for the most part, our community is very open-minded and supportive. You'll see at the fundraiser. Is your mom going to have a food stall?"

"No way!"

Mel shook her head. "Speaking of idiots…" She gave Shivani a quick hug. "But I like you anyway. Good night!"

"Bye-bye, Mel!" Ma called from the doorway.

"Bye, Aunty!" said Mel, grinning. "See you soon."

When Shivani went back inside, Ma was humming a tune as she cleared the table.

"Ma, you go rest. I'll do this," said Shivani. "Dinner was great! Mel loved it."

"So, I told you," Ma said.

"Yes, you did," admitted Shivani. Then she made Ma a hot cup of chai.

Chapter Ten

The weekend of the fundraiser was almost there. Shivani and Mel pooled their allowances for consolation prizes. It was Mel's idea to pile them at kids' eye level on the table.

"If that doesn't lure them in, I don't know what will," Mel said. "It would work on me!"

Shivani, who had never tasted a gummy bear before, tried a couple. "You're right!" she said. "I could eat these forever."

"And I could do the same with jalebis," said Mel. "They are so good! Are you sure you don't want to ask Aunty to set up a stall? Mom could totally arrange it on short notice."

"Can we please not go into this again?" said Shivani. "Maybe next year."

Mel muttered something that sounded like *yeah right*.

"Sorry, what?" said Shivani.

"Nothing," said Mel.

Friday evening, the night before the fundraiser, Shivani's stomach churned with excitement. And hunger. It was almost eight, but there was no sign of dinner. Shivani headed toward the kitchen. Ma and Anita were chattering softly in Hindi, bursting into laughter every so often.

"What's so funny?" Shivani asked, stepping into the kitchen.

Ma and Anita froze. The kitchen counter was littered with used pots and ladles. Shivani noticed a huge mound of chopped cilantro on a cutting board. It gave off an earthy aroma that Shivani loved. Beside it was a mound of tandoori chicken, cut into bite-sized pieces. Shivani's mouth watered. Ma's butter chicken was to die for.

"Food time already?" said Ma when she saw her. "How clock flying."

Shivani didn't bother to tell her how late it was. She stared at Anita, who was stirring a large pot on the stove. She hadn't turned to look at her. Shivani could tell something was up. Ma and

Anita had been acting weird all week, whispering and giggling. She didn't like being left out.

"Can I help with anything?" she asked.

"Please set table," said Ma.

"Maybe I could clean up?" said Shivani. "It's a mess in here."

"I've got it under control, Didi, but thanks," said Anita.

Shivani turned and left the kitchen. *Fine*, she thought. *Keep your secrets. I have better things to do with my time.* As she set the table, she thought about the next day. She'd have at least four hours of minding the stall next to Ryan. They'd bumped into each other during setup and had eaten lunch in the cafeteria at the same table, but this would be a lot more fun.

As soon as Papa got home, they sat down to dinner. As Shivani ate, her thoughts returned to Ryan. He was a sweet and friendly guy. Shivani was looking forward to getting to know him and his friend better.

"Pass the yogurt, please, Shivani," Papa said.

Shivani snapped out of her daydream. "Sure," she said. Only then did she realize she'd been munching on *gobi* parathas with yogurt and pickles.

"Why are we eating this when there's butter chicken?" asked Shivani, looking with amazement at Ma. "You know how much I love it."

"Just realized that, did you?" said Anita. "I win the bet!" she said to Ma with a wink.

"What bet?" Shivani asked. "What's going on?"

"Settle down now, girls. You don't need to shout," said Papa.

"You're so wrapped up in your own world, Didi," Anita said. "I said it would be ten minutes before you noticed what we're eating tonight. Ma said five."

Shivani's face grew warm. It was true she'd been very preoccupied the last couple of weeks, and especially today. "Not that it's any of your beeswax, but I've been thinking about the fundraiser."

"You sure that's all?" said Anita, popping a bit of paratha into her mouth.

Shivani glared at Anita. Ma ate her food in silence.

"So do we get a taste of the butter chicken?" asked Shivani. "Or are you preparing for a dinner party?" Ma did that sometimes. She would cook some of the dishes a day or two in advance. They always tasted better the next day anyway.

"Yes. Party," said Mom, nodding. "Now hurry up finish. I have much work to do."

If they wanted to have secrets about a dinner party, fine. It was too boring to get involved in anyway. She and Mel were going to win the award for earning the most money. The prize was a school ribbon and two movie tickets, presented in front of the entire school. Her cool factor would skyrocket.

Chapter Eleven

Shivani whipped open the curtains. The sun beamed at her from a cloudless blue sky. She hummed a tune as she took extra-special care with her outfit. She slipped on her favorite ripped jeans, a cream shirt and a denim jacket. For a moment she hesitated, staring at the *kurti* Ma had bought for her. It was a deep royal purple and was covered in delicate white embroidery—*chikan* work. *Embrace your culture*, Ma and Papa always said. If she did that today, she would definitely have the most unique outfit at the fair. The kurti would go so well with jeans and slip-on *mojris*.

Shivani shoved the drawer shut with a sigh. She couldn't help it. She wanted to fit in. Not stand out. Sometimes she wished she could be more like her sister. Not only did Anita wear what she liked, but Shivani could have sworn she'd seen a couple of Anita's friends wearing her sister's outfits too.

"Morning, Didi!" Anita said, stepping out of the bathroom, fully dressed and heading for the door. An early riser, Anita was ready way before Shivani just about every day of the week.

"Morning!" Shivani replied in a cheery voice. "Where are you off to? It's so early!"

"I'm helping someone out at the fundraiser," she said.

"Oh yeah?" Shivani asked. "Games or food?"

"Food," said Anita and raced out of the room.

After checking her hair again, Shivani carefully applied gloss over her pink lipstick. She had to look as good as possible since she was going to be working so close to Ryan all day.

Shivani's phone buzzed. Mel.

Meet you on the school grounds in ten.

K. See you soon.

Shivani took one last look in the mirror and stepped out of the room. Ma hadn't brought up the topic of the fundraiser since their blowup. Shivani was relieved. She did think it was most unlike Ma to give up so easily though. Ma could be very stubborn when she made up her mind about something.

Shivani would make it up to Ma by being extra nice when the summer vacation began. Maybe she would make her a cup of hot ginger-cardamom chai and give her a foot massage one Sunday morning. Or maybe she and Anita could offer to cook lunch and dinner one day so Ma could have a day off with Papa. Her parents had not had any time to themselves since they'd come to Canada.

Shivani raced down the hall. "Ma! I'm leaving!" she called.

"Okay, beta, have a nice day," said Ma, stepping out of the kitchen. She smelled fragrant, like a tiffin full of delicious food. But she looked a bit preoccupied, worried even.

"Everything okay, Ma?"

"Big day for you, no?" said Ma.

"Yes!" said Shivani. "I hope our stall does well. Don't forget, I'll be home late. All the volunteers have to stay afterward to help clean up."

"If you work hard, the rewards will follow," Ma said.

"Right. Okay, gotta run. Mel is waiting for me."

It was odd that Ma didn't even ask if Shivani wanted breakfast. Not that she could have eaten anything. She was too nervous. "Best luck," said Ma. "Break feet."

"Thanks, Ma!" said Shivani, giving her a tight hug. "Bye."

"It's all ready, Ma!" Anita called from the kitchen.

"Go, go," said Ma, almost pushing Shivani out the door.

As Shivani ran to school, she wondered who'd been invited to the dinner party that night. Probably the neighbors. They had been dropping major hints lately about how much they loved Indian food.

Chapter Twelve

The school field was buzzing with activity. Volunteers with name tags swarmed everywhere. The smell of popcorn, candy floss and donuts was all around. Shivani looked for Mel. She was excited about the idea of winning a prize if they did well with the balloon-dart stall that day.

She and Mel spotted each other at the same time and waved. Even from here, Shivani could see that Mel looked great. Her blond hair was freshly washed and styled. She wore denim jeans and a cool white peasant blouse. They had planned ahead and deliberately chosen similar outfits. That was another reason Shivani had decided not to wear the kurti.

"Ready?" asked Mel as she got closer.

Shivani nodded. "You bet."

"I've already dropped off the gummy bears at our stall. If nothing else, that should draw the crowds," said Mel. "Please don't let me eat them all!"

"If there are any left over after I'm through," Shivani replied, smiling.

"Mom said there are a couple more bags in the car if we run out."

"Sounds good. Once we're all set up, let's go scope out the competition," said Shivani. "See what they're offering and then decide on a game plan."

Mel laughed. "I like the way you think, Shivi-girl."

They checked in with the teacher handing out money boxes with change. They also got a roll of tickets and an instruction sheet. They headed over to their stall. A large board covered with tiny balloons was already on the back wall. Shivani and Mel carefully arranged the colored darts on the table. Then they set out the large bowl filled with gummy bears. Even if a kid missed all three turns, they'd still get a small prize.

People were starting to trickle onto the grounds, so they decided to stay put. Shivani sat with the money box and tickets. She and Mel would take turns selling tickets and handing out the darts.

The stall next to theirs was still empty. Where were Ryan and his friend?

Maybe they'd changed their minds. Shivani hoped not.

"He'll be here," said Mel.

Shivani started. "What? I didn't say a word!"

"You didn't have to. Your expression said it all."

Shivani gave Mel a hug. "You're the best."

"I know," said Mel, grinning. "But feel free to mention it as often as you like. And hey, one more thing."

"Yeah?" said Shivani, her eyes sweeping the grounds.

"No matter what happens today, don't forget we're here to have fun. And raise money for the school," Mel said. "So, um…I don't want you getting upset over anything."

"Why would I?" said Shivani. "We'll do our best, and if we don't win, so be it. Oh, look! There he is."

"Hi, Shivani! Hey, Melanie!" said Ryan. His arms were full of plastic bows and arrows.

He wore blue jeans, a white T-shirt and aviator glasses that reflected the blue sky. *He is so cute!* Shivani felt a bit woozy. She sat down on the chair and smiled. "Hey there!" she said, trying to play it cool.

"This is my friend Calum," said Ryan. A boy with dark hair stood behind him, holding a roll of tickets and a money box.

"Cal for short," his friend said. "Hi!"

Shivani watched Mel look Cal up and down. She could tell her friend approved.

"I was in the gym where the food stalls are being set up," said Ryan. "It smells soooooo good in there! Now my stomach is begging for attention. I don't think I'll last until lunchtime."

"That's why there are two of us at each stall," Mel piped up. "In a little while, why don't you and Shivani go grab something?"

"That sounds good," said Shivani, secretly pleased.

"Yeah, then maybe you and I can go when they get back," Cal said shyly to Mel.

Mel smiled and nodded. "I'd like that."

Within the hour the field was full of people. It was a beautiful day, and Shivani was glad to see so many families out enjoying the event. Mel handed out darts and explained the rules while Shivani took care of selling tickets and making change. She also made sure no one tried to sneak over the line to get closer to the board. Most of the kids didn't manage to pop a balloon with the dart. But Mel handed out the gummy bears with a cheery "Oh! Too bad! Why don't you try again?"

Now and then Shivani glanced over at the archery stall. It didn't seem to be as crowded as theirs. *Good!* She and Mel *had* to win this. Shivani started calling out to kids and their parents, inviting them to step up and try their luck.

"It's easy!" she said. "Even a baby could do it." That was actually true. Earlier a toddler had grabbed a dart from her big brother. Before the mother could grab it from her, she had thrown it. Somehow she'd managed to pop a balloon. Everyone started clapping, and the toddler started to cry. Maybe she wanted to do it again.

Around lunchtime the crowd outside died down as people headed for the gym—and food. Shivani glanced over at Ryan. He was patiently showing a kid how to use the bow and arrow.

"Shivani! Wake up!" Mel's voice cut through her daydreaming.

A couple of people were holding out money.

"Sorry!" she said. "The sun got in my eye! How many tickets?"

Mel snorted.

Shivani noticed that people walking past their stall were balancing paper plates and bowls full of food. For a moment Shivani was sure she could smell butter chicken. Her skin chilled despite the hot afternoon. No, it couldn't be. Her nose was playing tricks on her.

"So much great food," a student said as he walked past. "And that last stall at the back—man, I hope they come back next year. I've never tasted food like that before. So different."

Shivani stared as they walked away. One word stuck in her head. *Different*.

No, no, no, no, NO!

Chapter Thirteen

"You mind if I take my break now, Mel?" Shivani asked, trying to keep her voice steady.

"Sure," said Mel. "I got this." She stared at Shivani with concern. "Everything okay?"

"I think so. Not sure. Gotta check it out." She was babbling. Mel looked confused. "Be right back," Shivani said, grabbing her bag from under the table.

"Listen, Shivi-girl, take it easy, okay?" said Mel. "Don't freak out or anything."

"What do you mean—" Shivani started to say.

"Hey, wait for me!" Ryan called. "I'm starving, and I need food. *Now*."

Shivani forced herself to smile. The one time she *didn't* want him to notice her, he had. If only she'd moved quicker or slipped out the back, she could have avoided him.

"Sure," she said. She felt Mel's gaze on her. She wished she could take Mel instead. But someone had to run their stall. And she'd have to make up some excuse for Ryan. Right now all she wanted to do was confirm her suspicions. "What were you saying, Mel?"

"Nothing," said Mel, not meeting her eye.

Everyone was acting weird today.

"Let's go," said Ryan. "If I don't eat soon I'll die."

As they walked toward the gym, Shivani studied the plates of everyone they passed.

Normal.

Normal.

Still normal.

But when they reached the doors, Shivani knew her worst fears were about to come true. That smell was unmistakable.

Ryan sniffed once. Twice. "What *is* that? That is definitely not the lunch lady's chili."

Oh no, Shivani thought, her heart beating hard. That stubborn mother of hers had gone and ruined *everything*!

The food stalls were set up along the sides of the gym. But there was such a crowd that Shivani couldn't get a good look at them all. She didn't answer

Ryan's question, but her nose had confirmed her worst fears. Despite her begging Ma not to embarrass her, she'd gone ahead and set up her food stall anyway.

As Shivani made her way to the back of the gym, the last few days started to make sense. Being shooed out of the kitchen. Ma and Anita always giggling away. The butter-chicken sauce on the stove. They had been preparing for the fundraiser. And neither of them had let her in on the secret.

"Wow! Will you look at that line!" said Ryan. "There must be something awesome at that stall."

"Probably burgers, hot dogs and fries," said Shivani. "It's what kids love, right?"

"Shivani! There you are!"

Shivani turned around. It was Mel's mom. She smiled at Shivani and then turned her attention back to the paper plate she held. It was loaded with the food Shivani knew so well. There were a couple of mini *poories*, the delicious fried bread that Shivani loved. And two small paper bowls filled with *chana masala* and butter chicken. Mrs. Jennings was using a poorie to scoop mouthfuls of the two dishes.

"This is the *best* food I have ever eaten. You should try—" She stopped herself and laughed. "What am I saying? You *know* how great this is!"

"It smells *amazing*," said Ryan.

Shivani nodded through clenched teeth. She wanted to throw up.

"You knew Ma had signed up as a food-stall volunteer?" she asked.

Mrs. Jennings nodded. "I am sorry, Shivani. Keeping it a secret was Mel's idea. After she tasted your mother's cooking, she knew a Taste of India stall would be a hit. I agreed because I felt it was the perfect way to introduce your mother to our community. Mel said she would make you understand. And there she is."

Mel came running up to them. Mrs. Jennings moved on.

Shivani pulled Mel aside. "How could you?" she said, making sure Ryan didn't overhear. "I thought you were my friend!"

"Sorry, Shivi-girl," said Mel. "But I knew you wouldn't agree. Even Aunty was reluctant to do this without telling you. But I knew this was the only way."

"And now everyone is going to laugh at me. And at my mother," said Shivani, choking back tears. "She wasn't ready for this yet."

Mel looked over Shivani's shoulder. "Well, why don't we go check out how *terribly* your mom is doing. Then I'll make it up to you, any way I can."

"C'mon, let's get going," said Ryan, interrupting. "My taste buds are going crazy."

"Hey, who's looking after our stall?" said Shivani.

"I asked Katya," said Mel. "She seems pretty cool."

Shivani followed the line to the back of the gym. People were inching forward slowly.

"This food is to die for," she heard an old lady say.

"I'm here for thirds," a teen said to his friend. "You gotta try this, bro."

Finally she reached the head of the line. And there they were. Ma was handing out loaded plates while Anita collected the money. They moved quickly. What was slowing down the line were the people asking for selfies with Ma and Anita.

Ma was wearing a beautiful green sari embroidered with peacocks.

Anita wore a sunshine-yellow shalwar kameez. They must have changed after Shivani left. She looked back at the line of people. They were snapping pictures of her family even as they waited.

"May I take a picture with you?" Shivani heard a parent ask.

Ma nodded, smiling. "You take," she said and posed with a plate of food.

"Thank you!"

It happened again and again.

"Hey, you two," said Shivani, approaching the stall.

"Hello, beta," said Ma. "No talk now. At home, okay?" She noticed Mel come up behind Shivi. "Hello, Melanie, we doing good, no?"

"Doing *great*, yes!"

Anita looked up at Mel. "We're almost out of food! Papa is on his way with the next batch. We did it, Mel!"

Someone touched Shivani's elbow. Ryan. She'd forgotten he was here!

Shivani cringed. Ryan's last experience with curry had not gone well. What must he be thinking now?

"Hey, do you think you could use your influence and snag me a plate?" said Ryan. "I'll die of hunger if I have to stand in line."

Shivani stared. Was he serious? Or was he making fun of her?

"Please," said Ryan. "This is your chance to save a dying soul."

"And while you're at it, get one for me too," said Mel. "I'm calling in that favor you owe me."

Shivani was shocked. She looked over at Ma. She looked so happy. And she was making a lot of other people happy too. What had Shivani been so worried about? She should have trusted her friend from the start.

"Thanks, Mel," she said, throwing her arms around her best friend. "You're the best!"

"I know," Mel said, "but get us some of that butter chicken before we die."

Chapter Fourteen

The gym was crammed. Parents stood along the walls and at the back. It was their last assembly before the summer holidays. Principal Travers was going to announce which stall had made the most money. Shivani knew she and Mel hadn't won. The bouncy castle in the middle of the field had had a lineup three times as long as theirs. Shivani had seen kids going back again and again.

Anita and Ma sat beside her. Papa was working, but this time Shivani didn't mind. Everyone had loved Ma and her food. No one had even mentioned her halting English. They'd just raved about her mother's cooking. They'd told Shivani how lucky she was to be able to eat this food without needing to travel to the city. That Ma was lovely and that they were glad to have the Das family join their community.

The biggest surprise had been Ryan. As soon as Shivani scored some plates of food from Anita, Ryan had started eating. Shivani pretended to grab one of his poories, but he smacked her hand away. "Get your own," he'd said, mouth full of food. "This is all mine." He made sure to compliment Ma and Anita before heading back to his stall. Mel only said,

"I told you so" before hurrying back too.

Today, Shivani, Ma and Anita sat in the front row with Mel. Some people stopped to chat with Ma, and others smiled as they passed by.

The members of the fundraising committee and the principal walked up onto the stage. The buzz died down.

"It's a beautiful evening, so I'll keep this short," said Mr. Travers. "We've had the best year ever. I'm pleased to announce that we've raised a total of $7,310.65, far more than we expected."

The crowd cheered.

"Would you like to know which stall raised the most money?" asked Mr. Travers, smiling.

"Yes!" the audience yelled out.

Mr. Travers held up his hands, and the audience fell silent. "With a grand total of $1,997, the highest earning stall was…A Taste of India!"

What? Are you serious? Shivani sat there in shock. Everyone else was clapping and hooting.

"Would Anita Das and her mother please join me onstage?"

The applause got even louder as Ma and Anita stood up and walked onto the stage. Shivani was surprised by how proud she felt of her mother. And even of her sister. Sure, she would have loved to have won, but this was so much better.

Mr. Travers picked up an envelope and two school pins from the table. "That is the most money any food stall has raised since we started holding these fundraisers." He paused while the whole place broke out in more applause. "Anita, Mrs. Das, please accept these tokens of our appreciation. The envelope contains two movie tickets to any show running at the local theater.

Thanks to your efforts, we will be able to update our gym and equipment for next year *and* restock our library."

The applause was even louder this time than on the last round. Shivani clapped harder than anyone else. Her heart was ready to burst.

"Your mom is a superstar," said Mel. "Sorry. I didn't like keeping it a secret from you."

Shivani glanced at Mel. "I should be mad at you, but I'm not. Had you asked me, I would never have agreed."

"I know!" said Mel.

"Would you like to say a few words, Mrs. Das?" Mr. Travers asked.

Shivani held her breath. It was one thing to chat with a couple of parents at a time. But giving a speech in front of the entire parent-teacher community? Would Ma be able to do it? She looked pale. Shivani felt for her.

"On behalf of my mother—" Anita started to say, but Ma placed a hand on her shoulder.

"No help," said Ma.

Ma stood in front of the microphone. She patted the beads of sweat on her forehead with the edge of her sari. Shivani imagined herself up there, staring out at the sea of faces. Her heart raced.

"Thank you all," said Ma in a shaky voice. "My English not so good, so please to excuse. We new to Canada, but we want to settle up. We want to help, and this perfect time. I proud of my culture, my tradition and my food. I think you all like it too, no?"

More thundering applause. A chorus filled the room. "*YES!*"

Ma beamed, and her voice grew stronger. "Only thing I say is, never be ashamed of who you be. Be proud, and others will join you." She looked right at Shivani.

Everyone onstage was nodding.

Ma smiled and folded her hands in a *namaste* gesture. "Thank you for honoring Das family."

She got a standing ovation. As Ma and Anita made their way off the stage, Shivani watched them with a lump in her throat. The things she'd been hiding were what had endeared her family to their new community.

"I'm so proud of you, Ma. You too, Anita," said Shivani.

"Thank you, beta," said Ma, kissing Shivani's forehead. "I do this for you both."

Mr. Travers strode up to them. "Hold on a second. I'm afraid there is one important thing that has been overlooked. As principal of this school it is my duty to remind you of something."

"Please to tell," said Ma, looking worried.

"You have forgotten to invite me over for dinner," Mr. Travers said with a big smile.

Ma laughed. *Whew!* thought Shivani.

"Me too," said Mel's mother, joining their group. "My daughter can't stop raving about your desserts. I can't wait!"

"You are welcome, always," said Ma.

This summer was going to be spectacular, thought Shivani. They really had *settled up* in Canada.

She should have embraced the chicken a lot sooner.

RECIPES

BUTTER CHICKEN

It would take a couple of days to make this dish from scratch the authentic way. But here's a quick and easy version you can whip up on a school night.

Serves 4

Ingredients:

- 2 tsp oil
- 6 boneless chicken thighs, cut into bite-sized pieces
- 1 tsp ginger-garlic paste
- ½ tsp garam masala powder
- ½ tsp dry fenugreek leaves
- 1 jar of Patak's Light Butter Chicken Cooking Sauce (15 oz)
- ¼ cup water
- ¼ cup heavy cream
- Salt to taste

Directions:

Heat oil in a nonstick pan on medium heat. Add chicken and fry until lightly browned.

Add the ginger-garlic paste, garam masala powder and fenugreek leaves. Fry for a minute, until masala is aromatic. *Do not let it burn.*

Add the cooking sauce to the chicken. Add ¼ cup water if the sauce is too thick. Mix well. Cover and simmer on low heat for 10 minutes, until chicken is thoroughly cooked. *Stir regularly to avoid sticking or burning.*

Turn off heat. Add cream and mix well. Add salt to taste.

Serve hot with *naan* or poories.

CHANA MASALA
Serves 4

Ingredients:
- 4 tsp oil
- 1 medium red onion, diced (1 cup)
- ½ tsp ginger paste
- 4 Tbsp Punjabi Chana Masala (dry powder—available in the Asian food section)
- 2 small tomatoes, diced (about 1 cup)
- ½ cup water
- 2 cans (540 mL/19 oz) chickpeas, drained and rinsed
- 1 tbsp ginger, chopped
- Handful cilantro leaves, finely chopped
- Salt to taste

Directions:

Heat oil in a nonstick pan on medium heat. Add diced onion and fry until lightly browned.

Add ginger paste and fry for 1 minute.

Add the dry chana masala powder, and fry until it starts smelling great. Put in a little more oil if you find the masala is sticking to bottom of pan. *It should not burn.*

Add tomatoes, reduce heat, and simmer until mixture is a smooth paste. Stir frequently. Add water and mix well.

Add chickpeas to the sauce. Lower heat and let simmer for 20 minutes, stirring occasionally. Turn off the heat.

Add chopped ginger and chopped cilantro, and mix well. Add salt to taste.

Serve hot with naan, poories or basmati rice.

Acknowledgments

Thanks to my family and friends, who have always been supportive, especially Rahul and Aftab. A shout-out to my critique partners, Deborah Kerbel, Frieda Wishinsky, Helaine Becker and Karen Krossing. A special thank-you to my fabulous and patient editor, Tanya Trafford. And a heartfelt thank-you to the entire team at Orca.

Mahtab Narsimhan is the award-winning author of several books for young readers, including *Mission Mumbai*, *The Tiffin* and *The Third Eye*, which won the Silver Birch Award. Mahtab lives in Vancouver, British Columbia, with her husband, son and golden retriever. For more information, visit mahtabnarsimhan.com.

Titles in the Series

Orca currents

For more information on all the books
in the Orca Currents series, please visit
orcabook.com.